I Belong

Confirmation

Leaders' Guide

I Belong Confirmation
Confirmation Programme

Published by Redemptorist Publications

Text by Aileen Urquhart
Illustration and Design by Lis Davis

I Belong Confirmation first published April 2001
Reprinted June 2003

ISBN 0 85231 231 8

Nihil Obstat:
Canon Cyril Murtagh, M.A., S.T.L.
Censor Deputatus

Imprimatur + Crispian Hollis
Episcopus Portus Magni
Portus Magni April 2001

Printed by East Central One Media Limited

Redemptorist
PUBLICATIONS

Alphonsus House Chawton Hampshire GU34 3HQ
Telephone 01420 88222   Fax 01420 88805
rp@ShineOnline.net   www.ShineOnline.net

Dear Catechist,

Welcome to 'I Belong'! Whether you are an old hand at catechesis, or are just starting out on a new venture, you might be interested to know about the thinking behind this programme, and how it works in one parish.

It seems to me that spirituality, to be valid, has to be grounded in the reality in which we live. This reality is what we see, hear and touch in our daily lives, as well as the overarching reality of "what the eye has not seen, nor ear heard, nor the heart of man conceived". 1 Corinthians 2:9
Genuine spirituality will accept both realities at white-hot heat, and find that somehow they are fused (confused seems the wrong word) and that the very dirt we walk on is Holy Ground indeed.

Everyday Experience
This programme is therefore very much based on everyday experience, and encourages the children and parents to find the deeper realities behind everyday experiences. During each session with the parents, and then with the children, the catechists explore one of the themes.

The themes are ones that unfold naturally during the celebration of Cofirmation, and extra light is shed on them by looking at the Bible. But the themes start and finish with everyday experience. Hopefully the second look at them will be enriched by everything we share about Confirmation, Church and Bible during the session.

Communication
In a parish where there are several catechists it is very important for the leaders to meet together regularly. Not only will you have practical details that need communicating, but more important you will have a wonderful opportunity to get to grips with the theme by hearing other people's insights and difficulties. After all, catechists are not 'a race set apart' and the things you come up with will almost certainly be what is on the minds of the parents and children. Meeting together will make sure your catechesis is on the right wavelength and hopefully you will have an enjoyable hour or two in each other's company!

The beauty of basing the sessions on personal experience is that there are no right or wrong answers. If someone says he has never experienced the glory of God's presence this is a valid comment. If someone says she gasps in wonder every time she sees a rainbow this is valid also. In this instance the task of the catechist is to enable the group to reach, a greater understanding of the glory of God. Listening to one another, to what the Bible says, what the Church says, listening to the Spirit stirring within us, will bring about the understanding. An understanding of the heart more than one of the intellect.

Your own spiritual life
Of course, knowledge is necessary, and it is important to know what the Bible and the Church are saying to us. Reading the Bible prayerfully is very important. The documents of Vatican II and the New Catechism are very enlightening as to what the Church is saying. A useful additional resource is the General Directory for Catechesis. You probably have your own selection of good spiritual writers that inspire you.

Above all, it is important to PRAY. If you are busy, and most people are these days, it is easy to put off any serious attempt at prayer, and just get by with a few quick words and a promise to 'do better tomorrow'. I find that tomorrow is just as busy as today, and my life is a series of promises to God. However I still believe that prayer is the most important thing a person can do to improve the quality of teaching. I am going to stop making promises to God, and actually spend some 'quality' time praying now!

I hope you enjoy using 'I Belong'. I hope it helps you, the team, parents and children, to grow in the love of God. After all, this is what is at the heart of our faith, isn't it?

God bless your work.

Aileen B. Urquhart

Introduction

I Belong is a preparation journey for children who are receiving the Sacrament of Confirmation at 9-10 years of age as part of their reception of the Sacraments of Initiation. All the material is firmly grounded in the Bible and in the Catechism of the Catholic Church and full references are given for your preparation of each section.

In each section the children will be exploring one of the main themes connected with Confirmation. They will start by looking at their ordinary experiences of the theme and then go on to think about the theme in Scripture and in the Church. Finally, they will look again at everyday experiences and hopefully discover how confirmation is about REAL LIFE.

Contents

SESSION 1 — *Tongues of Fire*

a) Read Parents' sheet for background information on topic.

b) A bible to show children would be useful.

c) Coloured pencils may be wiser than felt tips for the children to use, as felt tips might show through. See how it goes.

d) If you are running short of time, leave all colouring-in to be done at home.

e) If you have time left over, colour in the title page, talk about Saint's names, practise the Sign of the Cross and the Our Father, have a chat with them!

f) Please be prompt for the Service in church, so no one is hanging round for too long.

Page 1   **Exploring 'fire' in their everyday life experience.**

If this is the first time you are meeting the children take time to establish ground rules of listening to one another, etc. The way you listen to them should set the tone of the session. Explore how fire can be warm and comforting as well as strange and powerful. It also played a big part in the development of the human race!

References: Old Testament some references to fire Ex. 3:1–6 (burning bush) Ex. 13:21 (pillar of fire) 1 Kings 18:30–39 (Elijah calls down the fire of God on the sacrifice).

■ **Parents' Book** Exploring 'fire' in their everyday life experience.
You will know what sort of experiences of fire your child has had. You could get across the 'transforming' element of fire by reminding him/her of cake baking sessions or food burnt on barbecues. Talking about not playing with fire will reinforce the concept of the power of flames.

Page 3   **Picture to colour in**

■ **Parents' book** Your child will probably not have had time to colour in the picture. Please encourage him/her to do so at home.

Page 4 Old Testament

A children's illustrated bible would be useful to show the children. It is not too important to know much about Ezekiel, except that he was prophet who heard God's word and spoke it to God's people. The children need to know what a prophet is, as through our Baptism and Confirmation we share Christ's mission as priest, prophet and sovereign.

The children cover the Journey in the Desert in more detail in the First Eucharist sessions.

Parents' book Ezekiel had many strange visions all given him by the Spirit of the Lord. The one the children are looking at is when Ezekiel was first called to be a prophet, about the time of the Babylonian exile. Ezekiel's vision makes him conscious of the immense difference between his littleness and the power and glory of God, but he is raised to his feet by the Spirit. (Ez. 3:12) and propelled on his Mission first prophecies of Ezekiel were ones of warning and foreboding, but the later ones are filled with promises of good things.

Another famous vision you might like to tell your child about is the dry bones which God can breathe life (Spirit) into. ('dem bones, dem bones, dem dry bones.') His final vision is again full of the glory of the Lord — God will dwell with the people, and waters shall flow from the Temple giving green vegetation and life to all. Even the Dead Sea will be full of life! (Ez 47:6–12) There is a similar vision in the Book of Revelation — the last book of the New Testament.

Page 5 New Testament

This page explores the difference between how God spoke to the people in the Old and the New Testament. People could see and touch Jesus only while he lived his earthly life. After the Ascension he remains with us through his Spirit.

References: New Testament more references to fire Luke 3:16 (John the Baptist [new Elijah] proclaims Christ. as one who will baptise with Holy Spirit and fire.) Luke 12:49 (I have come to cast fire on the earth) Acts 2:1–4 (tongues of fire) 1 Th. 5:19 (do not quench the spirit) Ad Gentes 4 (Pentecost overcoming the dispersal of Babel)

Parents' book The New Testament account of the descent of the Holy Spirit is the exact opposite of the Old Testament account of the 'ascent' of humanity to God in the Tower of Babel story. The Tower of Babel story is a continuation of the Adam and Eve story, where the first people wanted to 'be like God.' We CANNOT reach God by our own efforts.

When the people of Babel tried, their efforts ended in confusion and no one could understand anyone else. At Pentecost, the disciples waited for the promise to be fulfiled, and of course their hope was rewarded. The Holy Spirit descended, and unlike Babel, everyone understood everyone else. Instead of chaos there was creation — the birth of the Church.

Page 7   Picture to colour in

Page 8   Church

Although two distinct sacraments, there is a direct link between Baptism and Confirmation. The New Catechism says Confirmation perfects Baptismal grace, rooting us more deeply as God's children, incorporating us more firmly into Christ, strengthening our bond with the Church, associating us more closely with her mission, helping us bear witness to the faith in words and deeds. All the above is implicit on the children's page, but you probably won't have time to draw all the links out with the children!

References: Easter Vigil (fire, paschal candle) Prayer Come Holy Spirit … enkindle in them the fire of your love

Parents' book In the early church adult converts were baptised and confirmed by a bishop at the same time. They then received the Eucharist and were fully initiated into the church. Naturally parents wanted their children to follow in their footsteps, and gradually infant baptism became the usual custom. As numbers grew it was not possible for the bishop to baptise and confirm everyone, so eventually priests baptised, (and gave Communion_ and when the bishop visited his flock he confirmed.

This history has meant that thoughts about confirmation over the years has been very varied. Some people think that as it is a sacrament of initiation it can be performed at any age. In the Eastern Church babies are confirmed.) Others think that as it is to do with commitment the candidates should be mature enough to make their own independent commitment to the church. If your child is being confirmed before receiving Communion for the first time it means your diocese is following the original order of the three sacraments of initiation. The fact that your child is not old enough to make a permanent commitment should not worry you any more than it did when you brought him/her for baptism. St Thomas says 'age of body does not determine age of soul.' Also, sacraments are not something we do for God, but what God does for us.

Page 9 — Everyday Life

The stress on 'changing' the children is because fire is used as a symbol of the Spirit's transforming energy. Fire changes what it burns. Also, Confirmation puts a 'seal; or 'mark' on the children. They cannot therefore receive the Sacrament again.

Some diocese may not encourage the practice of choosing a second name at Confirmation, as they feel the link with Baptism is made clearer is the child's baptismal name is used. Make sure you know what happens in your diocese.

If a second name is chosen you might find it useful to have a book of the Lives of Saints to hand, as many children will not know who to choose.

References: Is 11:1–2 (gifts of the Spirit) Gal 5:22–23 (fruits of the Spirit) LG 4 & 5 (Holy Spirit and Church's mission in world) Catechism of the Catholic Church 956 (intercession of the saints)

Parents' book in many dioceses the candidate chooses a saint's name on being confirmed. This signifies their new responsibilities in the Church. The apostle Peter was originally called Simon, but Jesus called him Peter – 'rock' when he made him head of the church. Abram's name was changed to Abraham (Father of a multitude) when God promised him descendants.

If the name your child chooses is to mean anything it should be a name of a saint that your child could relate to. For instance, if your child loves animals, St Francis would be a good choice, whereas a child who is a bit of a tearaway might be inspired by soldiers like St Martin de Tours or St Ignatius. Find our about the lives of several saints so your child has a good choice. The catechist will not have time to help much with the choice of names.

Page 10

Explain that this page is theirs and they can add as much as they want to at home. They could stick in photos, make up prayers, do drawings, etc.

1st PARENTS' SESSION

Welcome.

- Discuss the parents' experience of 'fire'. Their most frightening experience, the time they felt most comforted by fire. They could brainstorm words connected with fire, and see which of them could apply to God also. As fire symbolises the transforming energy of the Holy Spirit, anything to do with the power of fire to change things could be stressed.

- **When the Holy Spirit came to the disciples they were transformed. They left the Upper Room and spread the Good News like wildfire!**

- What good news have we ever had, that has been so 'hot' we can't keep it to ourselves? (The parents will probably say things like the birth of their child, passing exams, getting a job.)

- **Do we feel the same about the Good News the Church tells us?**

- If we could only pass on one part of the Gospel message to our children, a part that makes our hearts 'burn within us' which part would you choose?
  What would be the comforting aspect of this message?
  What aspect would be fearful?
  If we really took the message to heart how would it transform our lives?

- **At home you might like to discuss the reading from the Acts in the children's book. See what is comforting in it, what is challenging, and see if it could 'transform' your lives in any way.**

- At this meeting there will have to be a lot of practical information given about the actual reception of the sacrament.

- **The parents also need to know early on that their child will need a SPONSOR, preferably their baptismal sponsor, so the link with Baptism is clear. As the sponsor undertakes to be responsible for helping the child fulfil his/her baptismal promises s/he should be mature enough to make this commitment, and should be confirmed. During the Confirmation liturgy the sponsor presents the child to the bishop (or minister), placing his/her right hand on the child's right shoulder.**

SESSION 2 — *The Oil of Gladness*

The Oil of Gladness

Read Parents' sheet for more background information on topic.

Page 11

The Oil of Gladness

■ **Parents' book** Talk about the things in the picture.

Page 12   **Everyday Life**

Exploring 'oil' in their everyday life experience.
As the children talk try to remember the words they use so you can refer back to them when making links with the Holy Spirit.
References: Catechism of the Catholic Church 1293 (uses of oil)

■ **Parents' book** Exploring 'oil' in their everyday life experience.) You might like to make a collection of all the 'oils' in the house and sort them according to use. The children's page on 'everyday life' lists possible uses.

Page 14   **Old Testament**

Whereas 'fire' is a useful symbol denoting transformation, oil is connected with peace. The Biblical references are given at the end of this section.

a) The children probably know about the Flood already. Although part of this story is to do with the reality of evil in the world, and how abhorrent it is to a good God, don't dwell on this. Stress instead the forgiving nature of God who renews everything, and promises to care for us forever.

b) The children may be pleased to know that God's chosen one was not the eldest or the strongest. They will probably be able to

identify with David, as they have had many experiences when they are conscious of being young, weak, powerless. Hearing that God doesn't go by outward appearances is very consoling, for only God knows our deep inner reality — that part of us is so precious and unique it is impossible to see or express.

References: Gen 8:6–22 (Story of Noah and dove with olive branch) Gen 9:1–17 (Covenant between God and Noah) Ex 30:30-32 (priests anointed) 1 Kings 19:15–16 (prophets anointed) 1 Sam 16:1–13 (kings anointed)

■ **Parents' book** Oil in the Old Testament often symbolises peace.

a) The dove bringing the olive branch to Noah signified peace between God and creation. After the flood Noah offered a sacrifice of thanksgiving to God, and God made a new covenant with humanity, setting the rainbow in the sky as a sign (to God!) of the promise. There are links with the first creation story (water, covenant, be fruitful and multiply) This is a new creation. Your child's spiritual life will be renewed at Confirmation.

b) In the Old Testament priests, prophets and kings are anointed. King David was the most noteworthy of the kings. He managed to unite for a time the twelve tribes, (North and South kingdoms) into one nation. The name of the capital, Jerusalem, means City of Peace. He was a Messiah (liberating his people from foreign tyranny.)

Page 16   New Testament

This page explores the parallels between the David's anointing and Jesus' baptism.

The paragraph on Jesus mirrors the paragraph on David. Draw from the children the similarities.

There are various interpretations of the temptations of Christ. For the children it is enough to think of them as temptations for an easy life. It is important that the children do know it can be hard following Christ.

(Take up your cross and follow me. Matt 16:24) but that there can be great joy in doing the Father's will. (My yoke is easy. Matt 11:30)

References: Luke 4:1–14 (Temptation in desert) Matt 16:24 (Take up cross and follow Jesus) (Also Mark 8:24 and Luke 9:23) Matt 11:30 (My yoke is light) John 18:36 (My kingdom is not of this world)

■ **Parents' book** The Baptism of Christ is like an anointing of him as King/Messiah. The word Messiah (Greek — Christ) meant anointed. When the voice from heaven says 'This is my Beloved Son' Jesus is being hailed as Messiah. (Kings were looked on as sons of God. Also — cf. Peter's profession of faith 'You are the Christ, the Son of the Living God.')

The Jews were expecting a Messiah who would be like King David and free them from foreign power. Jesus is indeed a king, but his reign is not of their earth as he told Pilate. (John 18:36) He frees us from the tyranny of evil. In the desert he experienced his own personal victory over evil. Baptism and Confirmation give your child this same power.

Page 18   Picture to colour in

■ **Parents' book** Once again, talk about the picture and see that it is coloured in. There may not be time during the session if a good discussion takes place.

Page 19   Church

Make sure the children know the strong link between Baptism and Confirmation. Confirmation 'perfects' Baptismal grace.

In this session we are stressing the Kingship of Christ, and therefore of the children. (You may prefer to use the more inclusive terms of Royalty or Leadership for the children). Point out the links with David, Jesus, and the children. David foreshadowed Christ, Christ is the definitive Son of God, Priest, prophet and king, but at Baptism we are incorporated into Christ. Therefore we also are anointed priest, prophet, sovereign. This anointing is 'confirmed' at Confirmation.

The sacraments are not magic, and the children may not necessarily feel anything on being confirmed. Other influences, e.g. family rows, or nerves may spoil the liturgy for some children. They most definitely won't sustain for very long any feelings of elation they may have during the ceremony. However, the sacrament does change and empower the candidates in a very real way. Help the children see the difference that Confirmation makes to them, and that this difference can affect their lives noticeably.

References: Catechism of the Catholic Church 1241 (Baptismal anointing with chrism/incorporated into Christ — priest, prophet, king) Catechism of the Catholic Church 1316 (Confirmation perfects Baptismal grace) Catechism of the Catholic Church 1295 ('mark' of confirmation) Catechism of the Catholic Church 1302–1305 (effects of confirmation) Catechism of the Catholic Church 1299 (gifts of Spirit as mentioned in Confirmation liturgy)

■ **Parents' book** There are real links between David, Christ and your child. All of them are gifts from God, God is their Father, they are beloved children of God, they are filled with the Holy Spirit, they have a role play in life which nobody else can fulfil. David foreshadowed Christ, your child follows him. Christ is the human being as God meant us to be: God's idea, the Word of God that was "made flesh" as Jesus Christ. At Baptism your child was 'incorporated' into Christ, coming to share with Jesus as priest, prophet, sovereign. This anointing is to be 'confirmed' at Confirmation.

Speak to your child about the JOY the Spirit brings. A sacrament can change us. And with Confirmation, this change is radical: we become full citizens of the Kingdom, the Church. We must all have experienced this strengthening in some way in our lives. Try to make the day of Confirmation one of great joy, and with this joy can come an optimism and confidence that 'with God all things are possible'.

Page 20   Everyday Life

Before you meet the children, think about the gifts of the Spirit and see where they are effective in your life. When the children tell you their favourite gift develop this by encouraging them to foresee situations where they could use the gift.

References: Acts 4:32–35)description of early Christian community) LG 12 para 2 (chrisms given for sake of church/others) Catechism of the Catholic Church 951 (chrisms given for sake of church/others) 1 Cor 12:4–11 (differing gifts of Spirit)

Parents' book After the highlight of Confirmation things will inevitably settle down to routine living. David was not made king immediately, but entered into the service of Saul (incidentally gladdening his heart with music) and Jesus spent forty days in the desert, symbolising the forty years the Israelites spent in the desert. In turn this symbolises our journey through life. But the Spirit is always with us, guiding us and providing us for life with great gifts.

Your child has these gifts through baptism, and they will be confirmed at Confirmation when the Bishop says, 'Be sealed with the gift of the Holy Spirit.' You will need to give your child gentle reminders of these gifts in the routine of everyday life. With your encouragement, you can keep the joy of the Holy Spirit alive in your child, so that s/he can cheerfully say with Christ, at home, school or wherever s/he is, 'The Spirit of the Lord is upon me — to bring good news.

Page 22

Ask the children to complete this page at home, and praise those who completed the last page of the 'Tongues of Fire' session. Do not praise for tidiness or good work, as this is not a test of intelligence. Also remember that some children may not be encouraged at home and may therefore be at a disadvantage.

Parents' book Your child could collect pictures of brave leaders or people who serve others with joy. A joyful family photograph would be also appropriate.

2nd PARENTS' SESSION

Welcome.

- Ask parents to name the most joyful person they know. Discuss whether these people are rich? Healthy? In employment? Have family? Friends? Have lots of leisure? See if there is any common factor. (If there is more than one group of parents they could write a list of what makes for a joyful person.)

- **Do outside circumstances make a difference?**

- Do they know anyone living in very 'bad' circumstances that still seems to be joyful?
  From where do they get that inner strength?

- **Read the gospel of the Temptation in the Desert. (Luke 4:1–12) Jesus was driven by the Spirit, (inner force) to external circumstances of deprivation. How did he succeed against the powers of evil?**

- What temptations do we have to cope with that correspond to the three temptations of Jesus?
  If you can, share with the group a time when you felt you were at rock bottom, but somehow had a superhuman (or supernatural) strength that helped you cope.

- **Straight after this gospel, we read that Jesus went to Nazareth and proclaimed 'The Spirit of the Lord is upon me... to preach good news to the poor, set prisoner free... etc.'**

- Your child is going to receive the gifts of the Holy Spirit at Confirmation and be enabled to share in the mission of Christ. As a family how do you preach the good news to one another... help one another see ... set each other free?

- **How can you enable your child to play a more active part in this spreading of peace, joy, freedom?**

You will need:
- **Samuel, David, Jesse, up to seven other sons.**
- **Oil.**

SERVICE   *Oil of Gladness*

Opening Prayer

Heavenly Father,
We have been learning about how your Holy Spirit makes us glad.
Noah was glad when the flood went down, King David was glad to bring peace
to his people, and Jesus was glad to do his Father's will. Make us glad to follow
Jesus and to bring peace and gladness to our families and friends.
We ask this through Christ our Lord. Amen.

Celebrant: *Reminds children of story of anointing of David.*
Asks children to come out and act the story.

Reading: 1 Sam 16:1–13

Homily

Themes of being chosen, gladness, dignity and responsibility of sovereigns.
Reminder of uses and symbolism of oil.

Children come up and receive anointing.

Catechist: Be glad that you are a royal child of God.

Child: Amen.

Celebrant: Let us offer each other the Sign of Peace.

Final prayer

Father you rule the world with justice and peace, and all creation sings your praise.
Help us to follow Jesus in the way of peace and be glad to do your holy will.
We ask this through Christ our Lord…

Final Hymn

Peace perfect peace (445)
Our God Reigns (244) or similar.

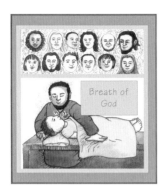

Page 23

■ **Parents' book** Talk about the things in the picture.

Page 24   Everyday Life

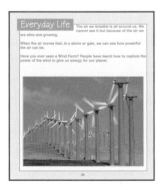

The concepts of air, wind and breathing are all introduced on this page, and they are linked with life and energy. Try to instill enthusiasm in the children. The word 'enthusiasm' comes from the Greek *entheos* — 'inspired of God'. God has breathed life into all creation. The children may have stories of sailing or visiting working windmills. Encourage a sense of gratitude for life / air.

References: Breath of God references Dei Verbum 9 (Scripture = speech of God written under breath of Holy Spirit) Catechism of the Catholic Church 691 (Spirit/ruah = breath, air, wind)

■ **Parents' book** We are inclined to take air for granted as we breathe it all the time. Try to raise your child's awareness of how life-giving it is by opening windows when the room is stuffy, or by having an invigorating walk on a windy day. You could also do an experiment to see how fire needs air (oxygen) by placing a glass tumbler over a candle and seeing the flame gradually die.

Page 26   **Old Testament**

As the story is quite long it might be better to read it yourself rather than let the children read it. They can then concentrate on the meaning. Stress the words 'spirit' 'breathing' and 'alive'. You could then ask the children all the things the child was empowered to do once he was alive again in preparation for thinking of all they will be able to do when they receive the Holy Spirit.

References: 1 Kings 17:8–24 (Elijah raises the widow's son to life) 1 Kings 19:11–13 (Elijah on mountain and still small voice) Exodus 19:16–19 and Exodus 24:15–18 (Moses on mountain & glory of the Lord) cf. Matt 17:1–8 (Jesus, Elijah and Moses on mountain)

■ **Parents' book** The stories of Elijah have a legendary quality about them. (Most cultures have stories, based on truth but embellished, that grow up round the national heroes.) Maybe Elijah gave the child artificial resuscitation? The story here is to give another example of breath/life.
Elijah was the great prophet who travelled forty days and forty nights to Mount Horeb (also called Mount Sinai where Moses spoke with God during the forty years in the desert) and found God, after traditional signs of wind, earthquake and fire, in a 'still small voice.' Moses and Elijah meet God again on another mountain at the Transfiguration of Jesus. Encourage your child to find times of silence, maybe at bedtime, because it is in stillness that the 'Breath of God' can most easily be heard. Give yourself the same necessary luxury.

Page 29   **New Testament**

Re-read the story of the Descent of the Holy Spirit which the children have looked at previously. Remind the children of the transforming power of the fire. They should be able to tell you why the Spirit came as a rushing wind. They might like to act being very frightened and disheartened, then excited and brave, full of enthusiasm.

You could develop the idea of the Birthday of the Church. There were all together as friends in an expectant atmosphere, there was fire (candles) and GIFTS. The idea of gifts is very important, as we have a tendency to think we can do things for God, all on our own, whereas we can do nothing without God's gifts. It would be worth reading Eph 4:4–16 before meeting the children. The author says we each have gifts, given to unite and build up the Church. To unite it as the Trinity is One God, and to build up into the maturity of Christ, the Head on whom the Body depends.

References: Acts 2:1–21 (account of Pentecost) Eph 4:4–16 (Paul's words on gifts of the Spirit for the Body of Christ)

■ **Parents' book** In Hebrew with word Ruah can mean 'breath, air, wind, Spirit.' One of the signs that the Holy Spirit had come was the rushing wind. A wind so powerful that a large crowd gathered below the house to see what was happening. The mighty wind reminds us of the first creation story in Genesis, where the rushing wind moved over the chaos and the heavens and earth were born. At Pentecost the mighty Spirit moved over the broken people in the Upper Room and the Church was born.

Page 31   **Picture to colour in**

Page 32   **Church**

The Mass of Chrism, generally on Maundy Thursday at the Cathedral, is a great sign of the unity of the Church. The Bishop is a successor of the Apostles, providing a link with the past, and priests from all the parishes of the diocese are also there, providing present day links. Representatives of people who are to be confirmed (and ordained) in the coming year present the Oil of Chrism to the Bishop. These, with the catechumens who present the Oil of Catechumens represent the future church. These oils are then taken to the parishes for use throughout the year.

This page spells out the unity with Christ which the Holy Spirit brings about. As we are changed into the likeness of Christ we share in his work. At their Confirmation the children can truthfully say, as Jesus did at Nazareth, 'The Spirit of the Lord is upon me, because he has anointed me; he has sent me to announce Good News to the poor, to proclaim release for prisoners and recovery of sight for the blind. To let the broken victims go free, to proclaim the year of the Lord's favour'. (Luke 4:18–19)

References: Joel 2:28–32 & Acts 2:17–21 (prophecy of Joel) Luke 4:18–19 (The Spirit of the Lord is upon me) LG 4 (Spirit sent to sanctify church/bring all to unity with Trinity) Catechism of the Catholic Church 690 (mission of Spirit = to unite us (all the world) to Christ & live in him) Catechism of the Catholic Church 702–716 (Spirit and Time of Promises) Catechism of the Catholic Church 717–730 (Spirit in Fullness of Time) Catechism of the Catholic Church731–741 (Spirit in Last Days) Catechism of the Catholic Church 1313 (Bishop = ordinary minister of Confirmation) Catechism of the Catholic Church 1297 (consecration of chrism on Maundy Thursday)

■ **Parents' book** When Peter went out to speak to the crowds he said the following prophecy of Joel was being fulfiled,

'In the last days I will pour out my Spirit upon all flesh,
And your sons and daughters shall prophecy,
And your young men shall see visions,
And your old men shall dream dreams...
And whoever calls on the name of the Lord shall be saved.'

This prophecy is still being fulfiled today. With Jesus ascended into heaven, and the coming of the Holy Spirit we have been 'pushed' into the 'last days' — 'the time of the Church'. The first days were at the time of the Old Testament, the time of the Promises, spoken by the Holy Spirit through the prophets. Then came the Fullness of Time, when Christ was conceived by the power of the Holy Spirit, lived, died and rose for us.

We are now living in the Last Days. The Blessed Trinity has been revealed, and we have inherited the Kingdom.

Confirmation, being another Sacrament of Initiation unites us more firmly with one another in the Church, and obliges us, even more than Baptism does, to work for that Kingdom. Jesus has given us his Spirit so that we (the Church) can carry on his royal, priestly, prophetic work.

Page 33   Everyday Life

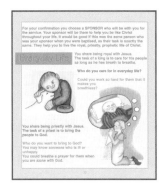

We have been talking about very wonderful things, and it all needs to be rooted in day-to-day living, or the promises of the 'Breath of God' will become empty words. Therefore encourage the children to give concrete and viable examples of caring for others in word and deed. You could draw three columns on some paper and put their suggestions under headings of prophet, priest, sovereign.

Explain that their sponsor is there to carry on with this encouragement throughout their life.

There is so much to say about the Holy Spirit, 'the Lord and Giver of Life.' The little bit you and the children learn is itself a gift of the Spirit. We have spoken about gifts, but most importantly we have the Spirit deep within our being, (as individuals and as Church) The Spirit teaches us all things. It is through the power of the Spirit that bread and wine the Body and Blood of Christ, the meal that unites us in love, and when we cannot pray 'the Spirit himself intercedes with sighs too deep for words.' (Rom 8:26)

'All over us all the Spirit is moving
All over us all as the prophets said it would be.
All over us all there's a mighty revelation
of the glory of the Lord, as the waters cover the sea.'

References: 1 Peter 2:9 (chosen race/royal priesthood) Catechism of the Catholic Church 908 (our share in Christ's kingly office cf. Phil 2:8–9) LG 10, Catechism of the Catholic Church 901 (we share Christ's priestly role) LG 12 (we share Christ's prophetic role) Catechism of the Catholic Church 768 (gifts to church for fulfiling her mission) Catechism of the Catholic Church 783–786 (People of God all share in the three offices of Christ) Catechism of the Catholic Church 1308 (age of body does not determine age of soul) Matt 11:25 (Father reveals to the simple — not the learned and wise) 1 Cor 1:27–30 (God chooses the weak) Rom 8:26 (Spirit prays in/for us) (Also under FIRE —Catechism of the Catholic Church 696 (Spirit as Fire) Under Anointing — Catechism of the Catholic Church 695 (Spirit as Anointing) Catechism of the Catholic Church 690 (The Spirit is Jesus' anointing)

Parents' book Just as God promised through the prophecy of Joel, the Holy Spirit will be poured out on your child, who will be confirmed in the power to lead with vision, to speak out against injustices, and to pray. As said before, spiritual maturity is not the same as maturity of years. The Spirit came to the young Mary and did 'great things for her'. The Lord said to St Paul, 'My power is made perfect in weakness.'

'Come Holy Spirit, fill the hearts of your faithful
And enkindle in them the fire of your love.
Send forth your Spirit Lord, and they shall be created.
And you will renew the faced of the earth.'

3rd PARENTS' SESSION

Welcome and tea.

- Make sure all the practical arrangements are in hand. These will differ from diocese to diocese. You may need to make sure the child has chosen and given in a card with chosen name, and that the sponsor knows what to do. (Right hand on candidates right shoulder.)

- **Give practical info. about places in church, time to arrive, etc.**

- **Go over ceremony briefly, linking symbolism to what they have been discussing at meetings.**

- Points to Make
  Renewal of Baptismal Promises. The parents made these promises on behalf of child at Baptism. At Confirmation the children will stand and make them by themselves.

- Laying on of hands.
  This, with the anointing, is the essential part of the sacrament. This is the sequence:
  The Bishop anoints each candidate by dipping his right thumb in the Chrism and tracing the Sign of the Cross on the forehead of the confirm and, at the same time saying.
  'N. be sealed with the gift of the Holy Spirit.'
  Confirm and: 'Amen.'
  Bishop: 'Peace be with you.'
  Confirm and: 'And also with you.'

- At this stage there could be a 'dress rehearsal' in church if the children were present.

- **If preferred the parents could sit in a circle round a table on which is displayed a candle and some chrism. Someone could read a passage from Scripture e.g. Isaiah 61:1–3. Then all sit in silence praying for the children while soft music is played. Some Bidding Prayers could be said, followed by the parents anointing one another round the circle.**
  'May the Spirit of the Lord be upon you.'
  'Amen.'

You will need:
- **Children to act as Elijah, Child, and Mother.**
- **Bowl of flour (bread rolls concealed inside)**
- **Jar of Oil.**
- **Red balloons with messages of Good News tied to end. e.g. I have come that they may have life. (If it were possible to hold this liturgy outside it could be very effective.)**

SERVICE *Breath of God*

Opening Prayer

Heavenly Father, you watch over us with love while we have been waiting
for the Holy Spirit. We have learnt about the tongues of fire, and have received a candle as a
sign that the Holy Spirit changes us and sets our hearts on fire with love. (*Light large
candle*) We have learnt about the Oil of Gladness and have received an anointing as a sign that
the Holy Spirit chooses us and strengthens our love. (*Place oils on altar as a reminder*)
Today we have been thinking about the Rushing Wind that was a sign of the new life the Holy
Spirit brings. Help our understanding as we listen again to the story of Elijah who breathed
new life into the dead child. We ask this through Christ our Lord.
Amen.

Celebrant

A reading from the First Book of Kings. (1 Kings 17:8–24)

Children to act our story.

Homily

(Reminder of symbolism of fire and oil) Talk about affects of Holy Spirit on
disciples — went out and preached to whole world – Three journeys of Paul, etc. Tell children
they are going to come up and receive a balloon with message tied to it.
They can release them for the wind to blow them where it will!
Children come up and receive red balloon.

Catechist: Receive this balloon and let it go,
as a sign you are to spread the Good News throughout the world.

Child: Amen.

Final prayer

God our Father, your Holy Spirit breathed over the waters of chaos to bring all creation to life.
We pray you will send the Spirit to us, so that we will be alive with your love, and have the
power to spread that love throughout the world. We ask this through Christ our Lord…

Final Hymn

'All over the World.' No 26 (Hymns Old and New)